Jeremiah 17:7 & 8

Contemporary Fiction by Susan McGeown:

Recipe for Disaster
Rules for Survival
A Well Behaved Woman's Life
The Butler Did It
Joining The Club
Embracing The Truth
The Best Secret (Coming)

Historical Fiction by Susan McGeown:

A Garden Walled Around Trilogy:
Call Me Bear
Call Me Elle
Call Me Survivor
Rosamund's Bower
No Darkness So Great
Windermere Plantation

Nonfiction by Susan McGeown:
Biblical Women and Who They Hooked Up With
Biblical Warrior Women and Their Weapons
Jerusalem Times:
JT: The Jesus of Nazareth Edition
JT: The Twelve Apostles Edition
God's Phoenix Woman
The Rise of the Mighty (A Study of Acts)
What We Believe (A Study of Romans)
C.S. Lewis & Me
Old Testament 101
The Parables of Jesus
A Book of Thanks
Prayer & Me
A Book of Blessing
A Verse A Day..

A VERSE A DAY

Letting God speak to you
one word at a time.

By Susan McGeown

Faith Inspired Books

Published by Faith Inspired Books
3 Kathleen Place, Bridgewater, New Jersey 08807
susanmcgeown@faithinspiredbooks.com
www.FaithInspiredBooks.com
Copyright November, 2018

ISBN: 978-1-946268-03-7

ISBN-10: 1-946268-03-8

Bibliographic credit appears at the end of this work.

Table of Contents

A Letter From Sue

Christmas, 2018

Dearest Sisters,

Merry Christmas, Happy New Year, and thank you once again for a blessed year of love, laughter, fellowship, and prayer support. Your presence in my life is one of God's greatest, most precious gifts.

Ah, the pressure to come up with this year's book! What will I do this time? I feared that I had run out of ideas. And then I thought of this one; thank you, Ruach, for the idea! Here is what you are to do with it:

1. This book is **not to be read in any order**; but rather "as the Spirit and your needs move you." I've even used different fonts so that different things may catch your eyes on different days.

2. Choose each day/time based on a random selection **or** what you need:

    a. Give me some **Wise Advice,**

    b. Remind me of my **Spiritual Power,**

    c. I need a dose of **Hope**,

    d. Show me my **Heavenly Father**,

    e. Remind me **Who I Am In Your Eyes**,

    f. I need a powerful dose of **God's Truth**, or

    g. Help me speak **Wise Prayers.**

3. Make sure to **mark what you have read** and possibly **make use of the blank spaces to write** your thoughts, praises, questions and answered prayers.

It is my hope and prayer that you will experience the rush of pleasure and joy that comes as the Spirit speaks to you each time you read these precious verses from God's Word. Remember, there is no such thing as coincidence; God is reaching out to you, calling you, speaking to you, loving you, and rejoicing in the relationship you are forming with Him.

All my love,

SUE…

Give me some
WISE ADVICE...

Study this Book of Instruction continually. Meditate on it day and night so you will be sure to obey everything written in it. Only then will you prosper and succeed in all you do.
Joshua 1:8

let us run with endurance the race God has set before us.
Hebrews 12:1c

Take delight in the Lord, and He will give you your heart's desires.
Psalm 37:4

But don't just listen to God's word. You must do what it says. Otherwise, you are only fooling yourselves.
James 1:22

DO ALL THAT YOU CAN TO LIVE IN PEACE WITH EVERYONE.
Romans 12:18

But I say, love your enemies! Pray for those who persecute you!
Matthew 5:44

We do this by keeping our eyes on Jesus, the champion who initiates and perfects our faith.
Hebrews 12:2a

Give me some WISE ADVICE ...

Fix your thoughts on what is true, and honorable, and right, and pure, and lovely, and admirable. Think about things that are excellent and worthy of praise.
Philippians 4:8

Give your burdens to the LORD, and He will take care of you. He will not permit the godly to slip and fall.
Psalm 55:22

Look beneath the surface so you can judge correctly.
Luke 7:24

Rejoice in our confident hope. Be patient in trouble, and keep on praying.
Romans 12:2

Give me some WISE ADVICE ...

Obey my commands and live! Guard
my instructions as you guard your
own eyes. Tie them on your
fingers as a reminder. Write
them deep within your heart.
Proverbs 7:2-3

*But I trust in your unfailing love. I will rejoice
because you have rescued me.*
Psalm 13:5

Tune your ears to wisdom and
concentrate on understanding.
Proverbs 2:2

Let everything you say be good and helpful, so

that your words will be an encouragement to

those who hear them.
Ephesians 4:29

Give me some WISE ADVICE ...

Give thanks to the LORD, for he is good! His faithful love endures forever.
Psalm 136:1

Don't repay evil for evil. Don't retaliate with insults when people insult you. Instead, pay them back with a blessing.
I Peter 3:9a

Think about things that are excellent and worthy of praise.
Philippians 4:8b

When troubles of any kind come your way, consider it an opportunity for great joy. For you know that when your faith is tested, your endurance has a chance to grow. So let it grow, for when your endurance is fully developed, you will be perfect and complete, needing nothing.
James 1:2-4

Give me some WISE ADVICE ...

BLESS THOSE WHO PERSECUTE YOU. DON'T CURSE THEM; PRAY THAT GOD WILL BLESS THEM.

Romans 12:14

Make the most of every opportunity in these evil days.

Ephesians 5:16

Be thankful in all circumstances, for this is God's will for you who belong to Christ Jesus.

I Thessalonians 5:18

Make allowance for each other's faults, and forgive anyone who offends you. Remember, the Lord forgave you, so you must forgive others.

Colossians 3:13

Give me some WISE ADVICE …

Don't be selfish; don't try to impress others. Be humble, thinking of others as better than yourselves.
Philippians 2:3b

Come close to God, and God will come close to you. Wash your hands, you sinners; purify your hearts, for your loyalty is divided between God and the world.
James 4:8

GIVE YOUR BURDENS TO THE LORD, AND HE WILL TAKE CARE OF YOU. HE WILL NOT PERMIT THE GODLY TO SLIP AND FALL.
Psalm 55:22

Fight the good fight for the true faith.
I Timothy 6:12

Give me some WISE ADVICE ...

BE QUICK TO LISTEN, SLOW TO SPEAK, AND SLOW TO GET ANGRY.
James 1:19b

But watch out! Be careful never to forget what you yourself have seen. Do not let these memories escape from your mind as long as you live! And be sure to pass them on to your children and grandchildren.
Deuteronomy 4:9

Don't copy the behavior and customs of this world, but let God transform you into a new person by changing the way you think.
Romans 12:2

Am I trying to win over human beings or God?
Galatians 1:10a

Who knows if perhaps you were made queen for such a time as this?

Esther 4:14b

The Lord is my helper, so I will have no fear. What can mere people do to me?

Hebrews 13:6

TRUST IN THE LORD
WITH ALL YOUR HEART,
AND DO NOT LEAN ON
YOUR OWN UNDERSTANDING.

Proverbs 3:5

Give me some WISE ADVICE ...

Remind me of my SPIRITUAL POWER...

And the Spirit of the Lord will rest on him – the Spirit of wisdom and understanding, the Spirit of counsel and might, the Spirit of knowledge and the fear of the Lord.
Isaiah 11:2

Now may the God of peace ... equip you with all you need for doing His will. May He produce in you, through the power of Jesus Christ, every good thing that is pleasing to Him...
Hebrews 13:20-21 (parts)

It is not by force nor by strength, but by my Spirit, says the LORD of Heaven's Armies.
Zechariah 4:6

The Spirit alone gives eternal life.
Human effort accomplishes nothing.
And the very words I have spoken to you
are spirit and life.
John 6:63

But when the Father sends the Advocate as my
representative—that is, the Holy Spirit—he will
teach you everything and will remind you of
everything I have told you.
John 14:26

**I pray for you constantly, asking God, the
glorious Father of our Lord Jesus Christ, to give
you spiritual wisdom and insight so that you
might grow in your knowledge of God.**
Ephesians 1:16b-17

Remind me of my SPIRITUAL POWER …

The Spirit of the Lord shall rest upon Him, the Spirit of wisdom and understanding, the Spirit of counsel and might, the Spirit of knowledge and the fear of the Lord.

Isaiah 11:2

LET THE HOLY SPIRIT GUIDE YOUR LIVES.

Galatians 5:16

When the Spirit of truth comes, he will guide you into all truth. He will not speak on his own but will tell you what he has heard. He will tell you about the future.

John 16:13

For the Holy Spirit will teach you at that time what needs to be said.

Luke 12:12

Remind me of my SPIRITUAL POWER ...

But you have received the Holy Spirit, and he lives within you, so you don't need anyone to teach you what is true. For the Spirit teaches you everything you need to know, and what he teaches is true—it is not a lie. So just as he has taught you, remain in fellowship with Christ.

I John 2:27

No one can know a person's thoughts except that person's own spirit, and no one can know God's thoughts except God's own Spirit.

I Corinthians 2:11

For I can do everything through Christ, who gives me strength.

Philippians 4:13

The Spirit who lives in you is greater than the spirit who lives in the world.

I John 4:4

Remind me of my SPIRITUAL POWER ...

But it was to us that God revealed these things by his Spirit. For his Spirit searches out everything and shows us God's deep secrets.

I Corinthians 2:10

And the Holy Spirit helps us in our weakness. For example, we don't know what God wants us to pray for. But the Holy Spirit prays for us with groanings that cannot be expressed in words.

Romans 8:26

And because you belong to him, the power of the life-giving Spirit has freed you from the power of sin that leads to death.

Romans 8:2

I am leaving you with a gift-peace of mind and heart. The Friend, the Holy Spirit will remind you of all the things I have told you. I'm leaving you well and whole. That's my parting gift to you: Peace. It is a gift the world cannot give. I don't leave you the way you're used to being left-feeling abandoned, bereft. So don't be troubled or afraid.

(John 14:27 NLT & MSG)

Trust in the Lord with all your heart and do not lean on your own understanding. Seek His will in all you do and He will direct your path.

Proverbs 3:5-6

Praise the LORD, you angels, you mighty ones who carry out His plans, listening for each of His commands. Psalm 103:20

Remind me of my SPIRITUAL POWER …

I need a dose of HOPE...

Forgetting the past and looking forward to what lies ahead, I press on to reach the end of the race and receive the heavenly prize for which God, through Christ Jesus is calling us.
Philippians 3:13b-14

Now may the Lord of peace himself give you his peace at all times and in every situation. The Lord be with you all.
2 Thessalonians 3:16

Guard me as you would guard your own eyes. Hide me in the shadow of your wings.
Psalm 17:8

The Lord is for me, so I will have no fear.
Psalm 118:6

The Lord is my fortress, protecting me from danger, so why should I tremble?
Psalm 27:1b

And though you started with little you will end with much.
Job 8:7

My power works best in weakness.
2 Corinthians 12:9b

I need a dose of HOPE ...

*For I hold you by your right hand—
I, the LORD your God. And I say to
you, Don't be afraid. I am here to
help you.*
Isaiah 41:13

You intended to harm me, but God intended
it all for good. He brought me to this position
so I could save the lives of many people.
Genesis 50:20

What shall we say about such wonderful things as

these? If God is for us, who can ever be against us?
Romans 8:31

**Wait patiently for the *LORD*. Be brave
and courageous. *Yes*, wait patiently for the
LORD.**
Psalm 27:14

I have told you all this so that you may have peace in me.
Here on earth you will have many trials and sorrows. But
take heart, because I have overcome the world.
John 16:33

You have not handed me over to my
enemies but have set me in a safe place.
Psalm 31:8

For we are God's masterpiece. He has created us anew in
Christ Jesus, so we can do the good things he planned for
us long ago.
Ephesians 2:10

Then Jesus said, "Come to me, all of
you who are weary and carry heavy
burdens, and I will give you rest."
Matthew 11:28

I need a dose of HOPE ...

The LORD himself will fight for you.
Just stay calm.
Exodus 14:14

Ask me and I will tell you remarkable
secrets you do not know about things to
come.
Jeremiah 33:3

Now may our Lord Jesus Christ himself and
God our Father, who loved us and by his
grace gave us eternal comfort and a
wonderful hope, comfort you and strengthen
you in every good thing you do and say.
2 Thessalonians 2:16

I need a dose of HOPE ...

These trials will show that your faith is genuine. It is being tested as fire tests and purifies gold— though your faith is far more precious than mere gold. So when your faith remains strong through many trials, it will bring you much praise and glory and honor on the day when Jesus Christ is revealed to the whole world.
I Peter 1:7

Come to Me, all of you who are weary and carry heavy burdens and I will give you rest.
Matthew 11:28

Don't be afraid, for I am with you. Do not be dismayed for I am your God. I will strengthen you. I will help you. I will uphold you with my victorious right hand.
Isaiah 41:10

Give thanks to the Lord, for He is good! His faithful love endures forever.
1 Chronicles 16:34

And we know that God causes everything to work together for the good of those who love God and are called according to his purpose for them.
Romans 8:28

SHE IS CLOTHED WITH STRENGTH AND DIGNITY AND SHE LAUGHS WITHOUT FEAR OF THE FUTURE.
PROVERBS 31:25

I need a dose of HOPE …

Show me my
HEAVENLY FATHER

"No eye has seen, no ear has heard, and no mind has imagined what God has prepared for those who love him."
I Corinthians 2:9

We know how much God loves us, and we have put our trust in his love. God is love, and all who live in love live in God, and God lives in them.

I John 4:16

God is not a man, so he does not lie. He is not human, so he does not change his mind. Has he ever spoken and failed to act? Has he ever promised and not carried it through?

Numbers 23:19

Show me my loving HEAVENLY FATHER ...

God's way is perfect. All the Lord's promises prove true. He is a shield for all who look to him for protection.
2 Samuel 22:31

This is the confidence we have in approaching God: that if we ask anything according to his will, he hears us. And if we know that he hears us-- whatever we ask-- we know that we have what we asked of him."
1 John 5:14-15

This is real love—not that we loved God, but that he loved us and sent his Son as a sacrifice to take away our sins.
I John 4:10

For all of God's promises have been fulfilled in Christ with a resounding "Yes!" And through Christ, our "Amen" (which means "Yes") ascends to God for his glory.
2 Corinthians 1:20

Show me my loving HEAVENLY FATHER ...

Christ is the visible image of the invisible God. He existed before anything was created and is supreme over all creation.
Colossians 1:15

God blesses those who work for peace, for they will be called the children of God.
Matthew 5:9

God … is fair and just, and He declares sinners to be right in His sight when they believe in Jesus.
Romans 3:26b

He will wipe every tear from their eyes, and there will be no more death or sorrow or crying or pain. All these things are gone forever.
Revelations 21:4

Show me my loving HEAVENLY FATHER …

The LORD is my strength and shield. I trust him with all my heart. He helps me, and my heart is filled with joy. I burst out in songs of thanksgiving.
Psalm 28:7

The eyes of the Lord watch over those who do right; His ears are open to their cries for help.
Psalm 34:15

The Lord is good to those who depend on Him, to those who search for Him.
Lamentations 3:21

God will do this, for he is faithful to do what he says, and he has invited you into partnership with his Son, Jesus Christ our Lord.
I Corinthians 1:9

Show me my loving HEAVENLY FATHER ...

I am the LORD, the God of all the peoples of the world. Is anything too hard for me?
Jeremiah 32:27

But anyone who does not love does not know God, for God is love.
I John 4:8

Jesus told him, "I am the way, the truth, and the life. No one can come to the Father except through me."
John 14:6

The LORD directs the steps of the godly. He delights in every detail of their lives.
Psalm 37:23

Show me my loving HEAVENLY FATHER ...

The LORD will conquer your enemies when they attack you. They will attack you from one direction, but they will scatter from you in seven!
Deuteronomy 28:7

So humble yourselves before God. Resist the devil, and he will flee from you.
James 4:7

But the LORD said to Samuel, "Don't judge by his appearance or height, for I have rejected him. The LORD doesn't see things the way you see them."
I Samuel 16:7

We put our hope in the Lord. He is our help and our shield. In Him our hearts rejoice; for we trust in His holy name. Let your unfailing love surround us, Lord, for our hope is in You alone.
Psalm 33:20-22

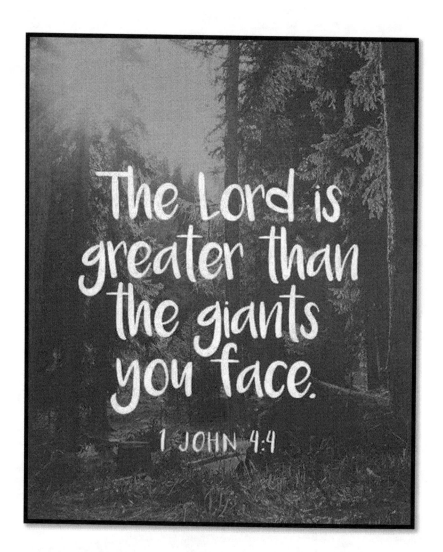

The Lord is greater than the giants you face.

1 JOHN 4:4

Show me my loving HEAVENLY FATHER …

Remind me
WHO I AM IN YOUR EYES

For we are God's masterpiece. He has
created us anew in Christ Jesus, so we can
do the good things he planned for us long
ago.
Ephesians 2:10

So all of us who have had that veil removed can see
and reflect the glory of the Lord. And the Lord—who is
the Spirit—makes us more and more like him as we are
changed into his glorious image.
2 Corinthians 3:18

THOSE WHO FEAR THE LORD ARE SECURE;
HE WILL BE A REFUGE FOR THEIR
CHILDREN.
Proverbs 14:26

Forgetting the past and looking forward to the future I press on to reach the end of the race and receive the heavenly prize for which God through Jesus Christ is calling us.
Philippians 3:12-14

People are trapped by their fear of others; those who trust in the Lord are secure.
Proverbs 29:25

But you are a chosen people, a royal priesthood, a holy nation, God's special possession, that you may declare the praises of Him who called you out of darkness into His wonderful light.
I Peter 2:9

MY SHEEP LISTEN TO MY VOICE; I KNOW THEM, AND THEY FOLLOW ME.
John 10:27

Remind me WHO I AM IN YOUR EYES ...

We destroy every proud obstacle that keeps people from knowing God. We capture their rebellious thoughts and teach them to obey Christ.

2 Corinthians 10:5

A spiritual gift is given to each of us so we can help each other.

I Corinthians 12:7

Let our roots grow down into Him and let your lives be built on Him. Then your faith will grow strong in the truth you were taught and you will overflow with thankfulness.

Colossians 2:7

But blessed are those who trust in the Lord and have made the Lord their hope and confidence. They are like trees planted along a riverbank, with roots that reach deep into the water. Such trees are not bothered by the heat or worried by long months of drought. Their leaves stay green, and they never stop producing fruit.

Jeremiah 17:7&8

Let your light shine for all to see. For the glory of the Lord rises to shine in you.

Isaiah 60:1

God blesses those who work for peace, for they will be called the children of God.

Matthew 5:9

With Christ as my witness, I speak with utter truthfulness. My conscience and the Holy Spirit confirm it.

Romans 9:1

Remind me WHO I AM IN YOUR EYES ...

Therefore I, a prisoner for serving the Lord, beg you to lead a life worthy of your calling, for you have been called by God.
Ephesians 4:1

Yes, I am the vine; you are the branches. Those who remain in me, and I in them, will produce much fruit. For apart from me you can do nothing.
John 15:5

"I will instruct you and teach you in the way you should go; I will counsel you and watch over you."
Psalm 32:8

We are citizens of heaven.
Philippians 3:20a

He replied, "You are permitted to understand the secrets of the Kingdom of Heaven, but others are not.

Matthew 13:11

For I want you to understand what really matters, so that you may live pure and blameless lives until the day of Christ's return.

Philippians 1:10

For in him we live and move and exist. As some of your own poets have said, 'We are his offspring.'

Acts 17:28

Remind me WHO I AM IN YOUR EYES ...

The LORD is my strength and shield. I trust him
with all my heart. He helps me, and my heart is
filled with joy. I burst out in songs of
thanksgiving.
Psalm 28:7

The LORD is
on my side;
I will not fear

PSALM 118:6

I need a powerful dose of
GOD'S TRUTH

But the gateway to life is very narrow and the road is difficult, and only a few ever find it.
Matthew 7:14

GREAT IS HIS FAITHFULNESS; HIS MERCIES BEGIN AFRESH EACH MORNING.
Lamentations 3:23

You make known to me the path of life; in your presence there is fullness of joy; at your right hand are pleasures forevermore.
Proverbs 16:3

If you confess our sins, He is faithful and just and will forgive us our sins and purify us from all unrighteousness.
I John 1:9

I need a powerful dose of TRUTH ...

The grass withers and the flower fades. But the word of the Lord remains forever.

I Peter 1:24-25

Don't just listen to God's word. You must do what it says!

James 1:22a

Submit to God and you will have peace; then things will go well for you.

Job 22:21

He must increase and I must decrease.

John 3:30

For the LORD corrects those he loves, just as a father corrects a child in whom he delights.

Proverbs 3:12

I need a powerful dose of TRUTH ...

We are each responsible for our own conduct.
Galatians 6:5

What He opens no one can close; and what He closes, no one can open.
Revelations 3:7

And I am convinced that nothing can ever separate us from God's love.
Romans 8:38a

If you are faithful in little things, you will be faithful in large ones.
Luke 16:10

I need a powerful dose of TRUTH …

"For I know the plans I have for you," says the Lord. "They are plans for good and not for disaster, to give you a future and a hope."
Jeremiah 29:11

Believe in the Lord Jesus and you will be saved, along with everyone in your household.
Acts 16:31

For this world is not our permanent home, we are looking forward to a home yet to come!
Hebrews 13:14

For God has not given us a spirit of fear and timidity but of power, love, and self-discipline.
I Timothy 1:7

I need a powerful dose of TRUTH ...

It is impossible for God to lie.
Hebrews 6:18b

Even when I walk through the darkest valley, I will not be afraid for you are close beside me.
Psalm 23:4a

For God loved the world so much that he gave his one and only Son, so that everyone who believes in him will not perish but have eternal life.
John 3:16

And it is impossible to please God without faith. Anyone who wants to come to him must believe that God exists and that he rewards those who sincerely seek him.
Hebrews 11:6

I need a powerful dose of TRUTH ...

Though the rain comes in torrents and the floodwaters rise and the winds beat against that house it won't collapse because it is built on bedrock.
Matthew 7:25

You will keep in perfect peace all who trust in You and all whose thoughts are fixed on You.
Isaiah 26:3

The earnest prayer of a righteous person has great power and produces wonderful results.
James 5:16

Jesus Christ is the same yesterday, today, and forever.
Hebrews 13:8

I need a powerful dose of TRUTH ...

Now all glory to God who is able to keep you from falling away and will bring you with great joy into His glorious presence without a single fault.
Jude 24

I WILL FORGIVE THEIR WICKEDNESS, AND I WILL NEVER AGAIN REMEMBER THEIR SINS.
Jeremiah 31:34c

A triple braided cord is not easily broken.
Ecclesiastes 4:12b

Anyone who belongs to Christ has become a new person. The old life is gone; a new life has begun!
2 Corinthians 5:17

I need a powerful dose of TRUTH ...

For the LORD grants wisdom! From his mouth come knowledge and understanding. He grants a treasure of common sense to the honest. He is a shield to those who walk with integrity.

Proverbs 2:6-7

Look at the lilies and how they grow. They don't work or make their clothing, yet Solomon in all his glory was not dressed as beautifully as they are. And if God cares so wonderfully for flowers that are here today and thrown into the fire tomorrow, he will certainly care for you.

Luke 12:27-28

A good tree can't produce bad fruit, and a bad tree can't produce good fruit.

Luke 6:43

I need a powerful dose of TRUTH ...

Those who live in the shelter of the Most High will find rest in the shadow of the Almighty.
Psalm 91:1

You know what I am going to say even before I say it, LORD.
Psalm 139:4

I give them eternal life, and they will never perish. No one can snatch them away from me, for my Father has given them to me, and he is more powerful than anyone else. No one can snatch them from the Father's hand.
John 10:28-29

Faith shows the reality of what we hope for; it is the evidence of things we cannot see.
Hebrews 11:1

I need a powerful dose of TRUTH ...

SO LET'S NOT GET TIRED OF DOING WHAT
IS GOOD. AT JUST THE RIGHT TIME WE WILL
REAP A HARVEST OF BLESSING IF WE
DON'T GIVE UP.
Galatians 6:9

Can two people walk together without
agreeing on the direction?
Amos 3:3

Where can I flee from Your Spirit? Or
where will I run from Your Presence?
If I rise to heaven, there you are!
If I lay down with the dead, there you
are! If I take wings with the dawn
and settle down on the western horizon
your hand will guide me there, too,
while your right hand keeps a firm
grip on me.
Psalm 137:7

The LORD is good to those who wait for Him,
to the soul who seeks Him.
Lamentations 3:25

But the fruit of the Spirit is love, joy, peace,

patience, kindness, goodness, faithfulness,

gentleness, and self-control.
Galatians 5:22-23

We can make our plans, but the LORD
determines our steps.
Proverbs 16:9

Who then will condemn us? No one—for Christ Jesus
died for us and was raised to life for us, and he is sitting in the
place of honor at God's right hand, pleading for us.
Romans 8:34

I need a powerful dose of TRUTH ...

But from there you will search again for the LORD your God. And if you search for him with all your heart and soul, you will find him.
Deuteronomy 4:29

IF THE WORLD HATES YOU, REMEMBER THAT IT HATED ME FIRST.
John 15:18

For since the world began, no ear has heard and no eye has seen a God like you, who works for those who wait for him!
Isaiah 64:4

I need a powerful dose of TRUTH …

JESUS LOOKED AT THEM INTENTLY AND SAID, "HUMANLY SPEAKING, IT IS IMPOSSIBLE. BUT WITH GOD EVERYTHING IS POSSIBLE."
Matthew 19:26

He personally carried our sins in his body on the cross so that we can be dead to sin and live for what is right. By his wounds you are healed.
I Peter 2:24

So where does this leave the philosophers, the scholars, and the world's brilliant debaters? God has made the wisdom of this world look foolish.
I Corinthians 1:20

Anyone who isn't with me opposes me, and anyone who isn't working with me is actually working against me.
Matthew 12:30

I need a powerful dose of TRUTH ...

How precious are your thoughts about me, O God. They cannot be numbered!
Psalm 39:17

For the angel of the LORD is a guard; he surrounds and defends all who fear him.
Psalm 34:7

Surely your goodness and unfailing love will pursue me all the days of my life, and I will live in the house of the LORD forever.
Psalm 23:6

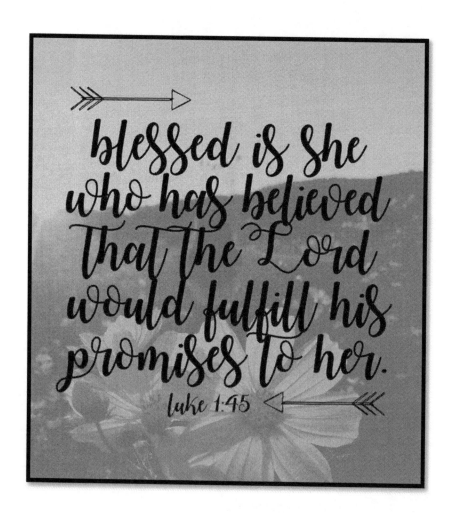

blessed is she who has believed that the Lord would fulfill his promises to her.

luke 1:45

I need a powerful dose of TRUTH …

Help me speak
WISE PRAYERS

Open my eyes to see the wonderful
truths in your instructions.
Psalm 119:18

May the words of my mouth and the
meditation of my heart be pleasing to you, O
LORD, my rock and my redeemer.
Psalm 19:14

The one thing I ask of the LORD—the thing I seek
most—is to live in the house of the LORD all the
days of my life, delighting in the LORD's
perfections and meditating in his Temple.
Psalm 27:4

Show me the right path, Lord, point out the road for me to follow. Lead me by Your truth and teach me, for You are the God who saves me. All day long I put my hope in You.

Psalm 25:4-5

Don't worry about anything; instead, pray about everything. Tell God what you need, and thank Him for all He has done … His peace will guard your hearts and minds as you live in Christ Jesus.

Philippians 4:6-7

Praise the LORD, who is my rock. He trains my hands for war and gives my fingers skill for battle.

Psalm 144:1

But I am trusting you, O LORD, saying, "You are my God!" My future is in your hands. Rescue me from those who hunt me down relentlessly.

Psalm 31:14-15

Help me speak WISE PRAYERS …

NOW ALL GLORY TO GOD, WHO IS ABLE, THROUGH HIS MIGHTY POWER AT WORK WITHIN US, TO ACCOMPLISH INFINITELY MORE THAN WE MIGHT ASK OR THINK.
Ephesians 3:20

I pray that your love will overflow more and more, and that you will keep on growing in knowledge and understanding. For I want you to understand what really matters, so that you may live pure and blameless lives until the day of Christ's return.
Philippians 1:9-10

Open my eyes to see the wonderful truths in your instructions.
Psalm 119:18

Help me speak WISE PRAYERS ...

I will ask the Father to give you another
Helper, to be with you always. He is the
Spirit of truth, whom the world cannot
receive, because it neither sees him nor
recognizes him. But you recognize him,
because he lives with you and will be
with you.
John 14:15-17

I pray that God, the source of
hope, will fill you completely
with joy and peace because you
trust in him. Then you will
overflow with confident hope
through the power of the Holy
Spirit.
Romans 15:13

Help me speak WISE PRAYERS ...

Lord, you are my God;
I will exalt you and praise your name,
for in perfect faithfulness
you have done wonderful things,
things planned long ago.
Isaiah 25:1

Help me speak WISE PRAYERS ...

About The Author

Susan McGeown is a wife, mother, daughter, sister, friend, aunt, uncle (don't ask), teacher, author ... but, most importantly, a "woman after God's own heart." Always working on a new book, she writes historical novels (including *Rosamund's Bower*, 2008 RCRW's Golden Rose winner in the category of 'Novel with Romantic Elements'), contemporary fiction novels, and nonfiction Bible studies.

She's been a teacher, a conference leader, a public speaker, a children's minister, a deacon, an elder, a vacation Bible school coordinator, a preschool director, and a Bible study leader (and recently she's become a seminary student!), yet writing stories is just about the best way she can imagine spending her time.

Living in Bridgewater, New Jersey, with her husband of almost thirty years and their four children, each of Sue's stories champions those emotions nearest and dearest to her: faith, joy, hope and love.

Philippians 1:20-21: *I earnestly expect and hope that I will in no way be ashamed but will have sufficient courage so that now, as always, Christ will be exalted in my life. For me, to live is Christ and to die is gain.*

> A WOMAN WHO KNOWS
> WHAT SHE BRINGS TO
> THE TABLE IS NOT
> AFRAID TO EAT ALONE.

About The Author

Bibliography & Footnotes

Thanks to these wonderful Internet sites:

www.biblegateway.com

www.biblehub.com

http://www.openbible.info/topics/

Thanks to these tremendous Bible translations that I regularly use and enjoy:

New Living Translation (NLT) *Holy Bible,* New Living Translation, copyright © 1996, 2004, 2015 by Tyndale House Foundation. Used by permission of Tyndale House Publishers Inc., Carol Stream, Illinois 60188. All rights reserved.

English Standard Version (ESV) The Holy Bible, English Standard Version. ESV® Permanent Text Edition® (2016). Copyright © 2001 by Crossway Bibles, a publishing ministry of Good News Publishers.

The Message (MSG) Copyright © 1993, 1994, 1995, 1996, 2000, 2001, 2002 by Eugene H. Peterson

New Century Version (NCV) The Holy Bible, New Century Version®. Copyright © 2005 by Thomas Nelson, Inc.

King James Version (KJV) (Public Domain)

Made in the USA
Middletown, DE
06 November 2023

42007381R00038